Vietnam Veterans Memorial
Remembering a Generation and a War

Patriotic Symbols of America

Vietnam Veterans
Memorial
Remembering a Generation
and a War

Joseph Ferry

Mason Crest
Philadelphia

Mason Crest
450 Parkway Drive, Suite D
Broomall, PA 19008
www.masoncrest.com

Printed and bound in the United States of America.

CPSIA Compliance Information: Batch #PSA2014. For further information, contact Mason Crest at 1-866-MCP-Book.

Publisher's note: all quotations in this book come from original sources, and contain the spelling and grammatical inconsistencies of the original text.

First printing
1 3 5 7 9 8 6 4 2

Library of Congress Cataloging-in-Publication Data

   on file at the Library of Congress

        ISBN: 978-1-4222-3136-4 (hc)
        ISBN: 978-1-4222-8759-0 (ebook)

Patriotic Symbols of America series ISBN: 978-1-4222-3117-3

Contents

KEY ICONS TO LOOK FOR:

 Text-dependent questions: These questions send the reader back to the text for more careful attention to the evidence presented there.

 Words to understand: These words with their easy-to-understand definitions will increase the reader's understanding of the text, while building vocabulary skills.

 Series glossary of key terms: This back-of-the book glossary contains terminology used throughout this series. Words found here increase the reader's ability to read and comprehend higher-level books and articles in this field.

 Research projects: Readers are pointed toward areas of further inquiry connected to each chapter. Suggestions are provided for projects that encourage deeper research and analysis.

 Sidebars: This boxed material within the main text allows readers to build knowledge, gain insights, explore possibilities, and broaden their perspectives by weaving together additional information to provide realistic and holistic perspectives.

Patriotic Symbols and American History

Symbols are not merely ornaments to admire—they also tell us stories. If you look at one of them closely, you may want to find out why it was made and what it truly means. If you ask people who live in the society in which the symbol exists, you will learn some things. But by studying the people who created that symbol and the reasons why they made it, you will understand the deepest meanings of that symbol.

The United States owes its identity to great events in history, and the most remarkable of our patriotic symbols are rooted in these events. The struggle for independence from Great Britain gave America the Declaration of Independence, the Liberty Bell, the American flag, and other images of freedom. The War of 1812 gave the young country a song dedicated to the flag, "The Star-Spangled Banner," which became our national anthem. Nature gave the country its national animal, the bald eagle. These symbols established the identity of the new nation, and set it apart from the nations of the Old World.

To be emotionally moving, a symbol must strike people with a sense of power and unity. But it often takes a long time for a new symbol to be accepted by all the people, especially if there are older symbols that have gradually lost popularity. For example, the image of Uncle Sam has replaced Brother Jonathan, an earlier representation of the national will, while the Statue of Liberty has replaced Columbia, a woman who represented liberty to Americans in the early 19th century. Since then, Uncle Sam and the Statue of Liberty have endured and have become cherished icons of America.

Of all the symbols, the Statue of Liberty has perhaps the most curious story, for unlike other symbols, Americans did not create her. She was created by the French, who then gave her to America. Hence, she represented not what Americans thought of their country but rather what the French thought of America. It was many years before Americans decided to accept this French goddess of Liberty as a symbol for the United States and its special role among the nations: to spread freedom and enlighten the world.

This series of books is valuable because it presents the story of each of America's great symbols in a freshly written way and will contribute to the students' knowledge and awareness of them. It it to be hoped that this information will awaken an abiding interest in American history, as well as in the meanings of American symbols.

— Barry Moreno,
librarian and historian
Ellis Island/Statue of Liberty National Monument

Words to Understand

etched—to produce an image on a hard surface such as glass or stone.

symbolism—something used to represent something else.

weathered—showing signs of life in a harsh environment.

A visitor to the Vietnam Veterans Memorial takes a photograph of a name carved into the long black wall. The memorial includes the names of every soldier who died in the Vietnam War. It is among the most visited memorials in Washington, D.C., with more than 4 million visitors each year.

The Wall that Heals

It is a warm spring afternoon in Washington D.C. Thousands of visitors have come to the National Mall to soak up history and explore the sights of the city.

A few people linger at the Lincoln Memorial, built in honor of the president who fought for equality among all men. Others stop to remember the contributions made by Thomas Jefferson at a memorial built in his honor. Still others gaze at the imposing Washington Monument.

By far, however, the greatest number of people stop at the Vietnam Veterans Memorial, a long, black wall sunk down in the earth, tucked away in a corner of the Mall.

A man approaches slowly, almost hesitating as he comes closer. He gazes at the impressive wall, and then hangs his head silently. A few minutes later, he

9

approaches the shiny wall, *etched* with the names of more than 58,200 men killed during the Vietnam War. His eyes search the rows and columns. Finally, he finds the name of a friend who died in the war.

The man reaches out toward the wall, his *weathered* hands trembling. His fingers gently trace the letters of his friend's name.

The man begins to cry.

It is an emotional scene repeated thousands of times each year. The Vietnam Veterans Memorial is a powerful symbol of American freedom because of all that it represents: the bloody struggle against a shadowy foe 10,000 miles from American soil and the intense reaction at home from people who had a hard time understanding what the war was all about.

When the Vietnam Veterans Memorial was dedicated in 1982, many veterans experienced mixed emotions. Although they had returned from the war years before, often the greeting awaiting them was anything but welcoming. The memorial was meant as a way to recognize and honor these veterans for their many sacrifices.

Make Connections

The names on the Vietnam Wall were grit-blasted in Memphis, Tennessee. Each letter is .53 inches in height and .038 inches in depth.

Many people hoped the memorial would be a place where veterans could find closure. It was nicknamed, "the wall that heals." Having a memorial built, in many cases, allowed veterans to reflect, to remember lost friends, and to heal psychological wounds.

While the memorial originally was meant to honor those who served in the military, it has come to have a profound impact on even those with no connection to the Vietnam War. Few visitors are left untouched by the *symbolism* of the memorial. The thousands of international visitors may know little about the Vietnam War and the United States' involvement in that conflict, but often they too are awestruck by the memorial.

Young people also visit the Vietnam Veterans Memorial. The connection for them varies, much as it does for adults. Many young people come to see the name of a relative—perhaps a parent or grandparent. These children have grown up recognizing the relevance of the memorial because the Vietnam War impacted some member of their family. For these children the role of the memorial is obvious. However, most children who visit do not possess such a personal connection. In the minds of many young people today, the Vietnam War is ancient history.

Text-Dependent Questions

When was the Vietnam Veterans Memorial dedicated? Why was it nicknamed "The Wall that Heals?"

Research Project

View a map of the original plan for the streets of Washington, D.C., at this Library of Congress exhibition: http://www.loc.gov/exhibits/treasures/tri001.html. Then, compare the map to a current map of the city. How has the city grown and changed? How closely does the current layout follow the original plan?

Words to Understand

Communism—a form of government under which the state owns everything.

corrupt—characterized by improper conduct.

oppressive—unjustly harsh and mean.

rebels—people who rises up against the government.

An American helicopter hovers over troops on a combat patrol in the Mekong Delta region of Vietnam, 1970. The Vietnam War was a brutal conflict that took a terrible toll on both the Vietnamese people and on the young American soldiers forced to fight in the war.

The Vietnam War

The roots of the war in Vietnam go back to the late 1940s, just after the end of World War II. For many years, the French had ruled Vietnam, a small country in Southeast Asia. But the Vietnamese people wanted to rule themselves. Led by a man named Ho Chi Minh, they began a fight for freedom, not unlike the U.S. war against Britain almost 200 years earlier.

It took nine years, but the Vietnamese people won their war for independence. Although the French gave up their claim to rule the country, it did not mean the end of problems for the Vietnamese people.

Ho Chi Minh and his followers wanted a government like the Soviet Union and China had at the time. But some citizens did not want such an *oppressive* government. At a special peace meeting in 1954, an agreement was reached to split Vietnam into two parts, with two separate governments. North Vietnam had a Communist government headed by Ho Chi Minh. South Vietnam had a government led by Ngo Dinh Diem, who had spent his whole life fighting against *Communism*.

Eventually, the two parts of the country were to be joined together following an election to decide whether the government of the North or the government of the South would rule all of Vietnam. But the leaders of South Vietnam refused to participate in the elections. They felt that the Communist government of North Vietnam would not permit fair elections.

It didn't take long for trouble to begin. Many people in South Vietnam did not like Diem's gov-

During the 1950s and early 1960s, the United States supported the government of South Vietnam, which was controlled by Ngo Dinh Diem. The leader of the North Vietnamese government, Ho Chi Minh (left), was a communist, and it was U.S. policy to oppose the spread of communism.

ernment because they felt it was dishonest and unfair. They favored Ho Chi Minh's rule.

By the late 1950s, a group of *rebels* known as Viet Cong began to fight against their own military forces in South Vietnam. Sensing an opportunity to control the entire country, the government of North Vietnam began to supply the rebels with weapons and soldiers.

Soon, there was an all-out war.

The United States decided to help Diem, even though his government was *corrupt* and many of his own people did not like him. One of the reasons U.S. leaders wanted to help Diem was because they did not want Communism to spread through Southeast Asia. If Communists ruled Southeast Asia, U.S. leaders were afraid the whole world could eventually fall.

At first, the U.S. sent only war supplies and a few hundred soldiers. These troops were supposed to teach the South Vietnamese military how to fight. Most Americans at the time had only a vague knowledge of what was going on halfway around the world.

But as the years passed, South Vietnam needed more and more help, so the United States started sending more money and more men. With no end to the war in sight, the U.S. stepped up its involvement in 1965 by sending troops to fight side-by-side with the South Vietnamese military.

At first, only a few thousand American soldiers were sent to Vietnam. But as the months passed, thousands more arrived. By 1967, more than 500,000 Americans were fighting the war in Vietnam.

Because of television, Vietnam was the first war that Americans could watch in their living rooms. Every night, people watched the news to see nightmarish scenes from the daily battles. They saw houses burning and wounded and bloody American soldiers. They saw dead women and children sprawled in the mud.

At home, Americans began to take sides on the war. Some believed the United States government had a responsibility to stop the spread of Communism. They supported the war effort and were known as "hawks." But others, mostly college students, felt the United States had no business being in the war. They were known as "doves" and favored letting the Vietnamese people work out their own problems.

As the war dragged on, there were more protests in the United States. The biggest peace march in history took place in Washington, D.C., in 1969, when more than

American doctors and nurses treat Vietnamese women and children in a clinic set up by the U.S. military.

Soldiers engage in combat with Communist Viet Cong guerrillas.

250,000 protested America's part in the Vietnam War.

In 1973, 14 years after the first American had died in Vietnam, the U.S. forces began to pull out of Vietnam. A peace treaty between the U.S. and the government of North Vietnam brought the fighting to an end. The last Americans left Vietnam in 1975, just as the army of North Vietnam took control of South Vietnam.

Almost 60,000 Americans died in the war and more than 300,000 had been wounded. Yet the U.S. government did not achieve its goal of stopping Communists from taking control of South Vietnam, a fact that caused many veterans to wonder why they had been forced to fight in the first place.

Text-Dependent Questions
Who was the leader of North Vietnam? Why did the United States support South Vietnam over North Vietnam?

Research Project
Communism is a political system in which the government (the state) controls all of the country's resources and factories. Explain how this is different from the system in the United States today.

Words to Understand

infantryman—soldier who fights on foot with rifles, hand grenades and machine guns.

scrutinized—looked at carefully.

subside—to sink to a low or lower level.

tangible—something that is real and can be touched.

Military police stand outside the Pentagon during an anti-war protest in 1967. By the late 1960s many Americans were unhappy about U.S. involvement in Vietnam. Unfortunately, because of anti-war attitudes, soldiers often did not receive a warm welcome home. Many veterans felt bitter that their country, which they had served, seemed to ignore them.

The Idea for a Memorial

A memorial in honor of Vietnam veterans was the brainchild of Jan Scruggs, one of more than 2.7 million Americans to fight in the war. A decorated *infantryman* and winner of the Purple Heart, Scruggs was one of the lucky ones who made it home from the jungles of Southeast Asia in one piece.

In 1979, 10 years after his tour of duty in Vietnam, Scruggs and his wife saw a movie about the war called *The Deer Hunter*. Scenes from the movie made him remember the dangerous days and nights in the hot, steamy Vietnam jungle. He once said of his service in Vietnam, "The bitterness I feel when I remember carrying the lifeless bodies of close friends through the mire of

Vietnam will probably never *subside*. I still wonder if anything can be found to bring any purpose to all the suffering and death."

Scruggs struggled for a year in Vietnam to escape the clutches of death. He now found himself committed to a different struggle, this one to enshrine the memory of those who fought so bravely and died in Vietnam.

In late 1979, Scruggs met with a group of Vietnam veterans in Washington, D.C. He expressed his belief that ordinary American citizens would donate money to build a memorial to those who fought and died in Vietnam. Some veterans thought it foolish to hold such a belief. Still, Scruggs persevered.

Scruggs and a group of fellow veterans formed the Vietnam Veterans Memorial Fund (VVMF). The objective of the group was to create a *tangible* tribute to those Americans who served in the Vietnam War in the form of the Vietnam Veterans Memorial.

When word got out that a group of Vietnam veterans were intent on building a memorial to veterans of the Vietnam War through public donations, members of the newly formed VVMF found themselves *scrutinized* and ridiculed. On the CBS *Evening News* one night, correspondent Roger Mudd reported that the organization, whose only concern had been about raising too much money, had gathered the grand sum of $144.50. A comedian on a network program made fun of Scruggs. The audience got a good laugh out of it.

Scruggs wrote "Our memorial had to be paid for by private contributions in a largely volunteer effort organized by people whose principal reward would be knowing they had honored those whom the nation managed to ignore." The Vietnam Veterans Memorial Fund soon discovered that many people, for many different reasons, would take a personal stake in the success of

VITAL FIGURE: Jan Scruggs

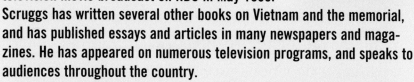

Jan Scruggs was raised in Bowie, Maryland. After he graduated from high school he served with the U.S. Army's 199th Light Infantry Brigade. After valiantly serving his term in Vietnam he came home and attended American University in Washington, D.C., where he obtained a masters degree in counseling.

After spearheading creation of the Vietnam Veterans Memorial, Scruggs wrote an emotionally moving book, *To Heal a Nation*, which is a story based on the Vietnam War and the making of the memorial. The book was turned into a television movie broadcast on NBC in May 1988. Scruggs has written several other books on Vietnam and the memorial, and has published essays and articles in many newspapers and magazines. He has appeared on numerous television programs, and speaks to audiences throughout the country.

Scruggs continues to serve as president of the Vietnam Veterans Memorial Fund (VVMF). The organization is currently developing an Education Center at the Vietnam Wall, which when completed will show photos and tell the stories of American soldiers who were killed during the Vietnam War. The center will also display some of the more than 400,000 items left at the wall, and celebrate the values embodied by American service members in all of our nation's wars.

In the summer of 1980, five years after the last Americans left Vietnam, President Jimmy Carter signed a bill that granted two acres of land for a memorial to Vietnam veterans. The land was located on the National Mall, an open area between the U.S. Capitol and the White House, which also contains the Washington Monument, Lincoln Memorial, and Jefferson Memorial.

this cause. A young girl who lost her father in the war sent $10. A vet with no job scraped together $5 and sent it to the committee. The parents of a young man who had been killed in the war sent a check for $25.

The fund-raising effort received a huge boost when Senator John Warner of Virginia donated $5,000 of his own money and helped raise another $50,000. Eventually, donations exceeded $8.4 million. The VVMF received private donations from more than 275,000 individuals.

Members of the VVMF decided that a site at the base of the Lincoln Memorial seemed perfect for their project. But the organization had to ask Congress for permission to build in that area of the National Mall. The wheels for site selection were set in motion when Jan Scruggs appeared before a Senate subcommittee with a briefcase full of documents justifying the site on the Mall.

The bill that granted the VVMF two acres at the foot of the Lincoln Memorial passed the Senate in just seven minutes on April 30, 1980. Two months later, on July 1, 1980, President Jimmy Carter signed the bill that allotted two acres of land, located under the gaze of Abraham Lincoln, to the Vietnam Veterans Memorial Fund (VVMF).

The veterans had their land. Now what? How could those who served in Vietnam be best honored?

Text-Dependent Questions

Who came up with the idea for the Vietnam Veterans Memorial? Where did his organization want to locate the memorial?

Research Project

During the Vietnam era (1958-1973), the U.S. government held a military draft. Young people between the ages of 18 and 25 had to register for the draft, and each year a certain number were randomly chosen to serve in the armed forces. As opposition to the Vietnam War increased during the 1960s, a growing number of young people attempted to avoid being drafted. Some refused to register with the government; others fled to another country, such as Canada, once they were drafted so that they would not have to serve. These people, nicknamed "draft dodgers," faced prison for violating U.S. law about participating in the draft.

In 1977, the newly elected U.S. president, Jimmy Carter, pardoned all those Americans who had avoided military service. Explain why this was a controversial decision at the time, especially among military veterans. How do you think that those who fought in Vietnam, and saw their friends killed there, felt about the pardon?

Words to Understand

contemplative—to look at something thoughtfully.

directive—an authoritative order.

guerrilla—a military strategy of using surprise raids to harass the enemy.

harmonious—agreement in feeling or action.

reconciliation—to cease hostility or opposition.

Maya Ying Lin, an architecture student at Yale University, submitted the winning design for the Vietnam Veterans Memorial. This is a page from Lin's winning design, which was one of nearly 1,500 submitted to the committee.

Designing the Memorial

The VVMF decided a nationwide design competition, judged by a panel of architects and artists, would be the best way to find a design worthy of this challenge. Bob Doubek, a veteran and co-founder of the VVMF with Scruggs, stated the purpose of the design competition: "The hope is that the creation of the memorial will begin a healing process."

Designing a memorial that could somehow help people heal their emotional wounds must have seemed quite a difficult task to those who submitted entries. Imagine the challenge of creating something that would not only honor the more than two million Americans who served in Vietnam, but that could also help the millions of family members and loved ones of the more than

58,200 dead and missing soldiers begin to heal. Could this even be done?

More than 1,000 people attempted to find a way. Those who submitted entries were given four criteria to follow in their designs: the design had to be reflective and *contemplative*, it had to be *harmonious* with the site, it had to be inscribed with the names of the dead and missing, and it could not contain any political statement about war.

With only those *directives* to guide them, 1,421 individuals submitted entries. After four days of closed-door deliberations, entry number 1,026 was the unanimous choice. Many were surprised to discover that the winner was a 21-year-old Chinese-American woman named Maya Ying Lin, an undergraduate college student at Yale.

At the time Lin was instructed to enter the VVMF design competition as a requirement for an architecture course. She had never experienced the death of someone close to her. Lin wondered how she would create a design that could help an entire nation begin a healing process. She visited the future site of the memorial on the National Mall to help visualize her design.

"I thought about what death is, what a loss is," remembered Lin. "A sharp pain that lessens with time, but can never quite heal over. The idea occurred to me there on the site. I had an impulse to cut open the earth. The grass would grow back, but the cut would remain."

Back at Yale, it took Lin only three weeks to complete her design.

Maya Ying Lin's design consisted of a long, black granite wall upon which the names of the men and women who had died in the war or were missing in action would be etched. It sought to honor their collective sacrifice.

VITAL FIGURE: Maya Lin, architect

Maya Ying Lin was born in 1959 in Athens, Ohio. An architect and sculptor, she comes from an artistically distinguished Chinese family that immigrated to the United States in the 1940s.

Lin attended the Yale University School of Architecture and graduated in 1981 with a bachelor's degree and in 1986 with a master's degree.

After designing the Vietnam Veterans Memorial, Lin cemented her status as a major figure of modern architecture with her sculptural design for the Civil Rights Memorial in Montgomery, Alabama in 1989 and a monument commemorating coeducation at Yale University in 1991. She is currently designing monuments and artworks that celebrate the journey of Lewis and Clark, as well as Native American culture, as part of the Confluence Project. The artworks are placed in public parks along the Columbia River and its tributaries in the states of Washington and Oregon.

In 2009, President Barack Obama awarded Maya Lin the National Medal of Arts. A statement from the White House explained that she received this award "For her profound work as an architect, artist, and environmentalist. Her vision for the National Vietnam Veterans Memorial emblemizes her deep understanding of the ways in which we respond to the world around us."

Initially, however, the design was not well received. A veteran assailed the design as the "black gash of shame." Other detractors criticized it as a "black, flagless pit," while others attacked it as being "unheroic," "death-oriented," and "intentionally not meaningful."

Supporters of her design felt that personal, political, or ethical reservations about the war could be set aside in order to remember and honor those who served. The memorial could begin the healing and *reconciliation* process of a still-divided nation. But before the nation could heal, old wounds needed to be opened.

The veterans were not new to wounds; they had suffered many. Serving in America's most divisive war since the Civil War, they fought in a foreign country against *guerrilla* tactics and an enemy that included women and children. Indecision and protests at home during the war gave way to indifference and hostility against the veterans upon their return. As they fought to make a life for themselves after the war, the veterans' shared experiences provided a common bond. Now, for the first time, they were divided, poised to inflict possible injury to that bond.

Make Connections

The granite used for the memorial comes from Bangalore, India; it was cut and fabricated at Barre, Vermont.

As debate raged over Maya Ying Lin's design, opponents suggested throwing it out and starting over again. Members of Congress registered their disapproval. James Watt, secretary of the interior in the Reagan administration, refused to issue a building permit for the memorial. Under the threat of losing their memorial, the veterans, their supporters, and their opponents met to find a compromise. They decided to add a statue and a flagpole. These would symbolize in a more traditional manner the patriotism and heroism that some thought was lacking in Lin's design.

In the end, the compromise of the Three Servicemen statue and flagpole fulfilled a purpose of the Vietnam Veterans Memorial–to help heal the nation's wounds. Citing pain as "a necessary part of ... the healing process for the wounds of Vietnam," a former design opponent, Milt Copulos, confessed that although "the wall of the memorial could have been a wall between us," it instead "became a bridge."

Text-Dependent Question
What architectural element was added to complement Maya Lin's design for the Vietnam War Veterans Memorial?

Research Project
In recent years, the U.S. military has fought wars in Iraq (2003-2011) and Afghanistan (2001-2014). Do some research to find out more about these conflicts. Then, design a memorial that would honor U.S. soldiers for their service in one of these wars. You can incorporate statues, columns, landscaping, and other design elements into your monument. Draw pictures of what it would look like, and write a paragraph explaining the significance of each element of your monument design.

Words to Understand

chronologically—telling a story in the order of events from the earliest to the latest.

repressed—kept under control.

A crowd of people gathers at the Vietnam Wall on the day the memorial was dedicated, November 11, 1982. The Vietnam Veterans Memorial continues to be, as the design jury noted, "a place of quiet reflection, and a tribute to those who served their nation in difficult times. All who come here can find it a place of healing."

A Tribute to Those Who Served

Since its dedication on Veterans Day in 1982, millions have visited the wall. Some come and make rubbings of names; some leave special mementos at the memorial, some simply touch the black granite and whisper a name.

But perhaps most important is what the memorial has come to mean. The wall is simple, thoughtful, and profound. It is a place to remember those who served during a turbulent time in American history. It is also a place for the nation to heal its wounds.

The Vietnam Veterans Memorial wall contains the names of more than 58,200 men and women who were killed or remain missing from that war. The names are etched on black granite panels that compose the wall.

The panels are arranged into two arms, extending from a central point to form a wide angle. Each arm points to either the Washington Monument or the Lincoln Memorial to bring the memorial into a historical context on the National Mall.

The wall is built into the earth, below ground level. The area within the wall's angle has been contoured to form a gentle sloped approach toward the center of the wall. While entering the memorial at ground level from either end of its arms, the descent to the center reveals more and more of the wall until it towers more that ten feet above the walkway. The center—within the protection of the arms of the memorial and surrounded by the grassy slope—is a place of quiet calmness and serenity.

On the granite wall itself, the layout of the names perhaps most strongly conveys the significance of the memorial. The names are listed *chronologically*, according to the date the servicemen and women died or were declared missing. Thus the story of the Vietnam War, from beginning to end, is recorded on the wall. Finding a name

Make Connections

The Department of Defense determines which names are placed on the wall according to criteria specified in Presidential Executive Orders from Presidents Johnson and Nixon. Those orders specified Vietnam and adjacent coastal waters, and later Laos and Cambodia, as a combat zone. Those who have died as a result of Agent Orange-related diseases or post-traumatic stress suicides are not included on the wall.

Each year, millions of people visit the Vietnam Veterans Memorial to find the names of friends or loved ones killed during the conflict.

would be like finding bodies on a battlefield, according to Lin.

The first name is located in the center of the memorial, at the top of the wall, under the date 1959, the year of the first death. The names continue line by line down each panel, as if each was a page in a book, towards the right end of the memorial. The names resume at the left end of the memorial and continue toward the center. It is here, at the bottom of the wall, where the last death is recorded, next to the date 1975.

As described by Lin, "The war's beginning and end meet; the war is 'complete,' coming full circle." By illustrating that the war has come to completion, perhaps the wall encourages visitors to move on to the next step of coping with their feelings about the war and those who served. In addition, the circular layout of the names may also suggest that the healing of the nation can also come full circle.

Other than the names, nothing on the wall describes who the men and women were. No name appears any more meaningful or important than any other. The

VITAL FIGURE: Frederick Hart, sculptor

Frederick E. Hart was a sculptor born in Atlanta, Georgia. He started out as a painter but was attracted to sculpture and decided he should learn the craft of stonecutting. In 1967 he got a job with the ongoing construction of the National Cathedral in Washington, D.C. Within a couple of years he was an apprentice stonecutter, rendering ornamental decorations.

In 1971, Hart opened his own studio to work out his ideas for the west façade of the cathedral, and in 1974 his design for the main entrance won an international competition. The finished work, carved from Indiana limestone in a tradi-

tional romantic-realist style, was dedicated in May 1990.

In 1981 his design for the Vietnam War Memorial placed third. In the uproar that followed the choice of Maya Ying Lin's wall, he was awarded a commission for a sculpture to compliment the memorial. His realistic bronze (pictured), known as Three Servicemen or Three Fighting Men, was dedicated in 1984. He later served on the board of the President's Commission on Fine Arts. Frederick Hart died in 1999.

names are distinguished only by how the men and women were lost. A diamond next to a name indicates a person was killed. A cross next to a name indicates a person is missing. More than 1,000 of the names on the wall are of people who remain missing.

The first additions to the wall occurred in 1983, the year after the memorial was dedicated. These 68 names were of Marines who were killed during the Vietnam War when their airplane crashed in Hong Kong. Fifteen more names were added in 1984. In 1986, 110 names were added when the geographic criteria were enlarged to include those who were part of the war effort but killed outside the war zone itself.

Since 1986, other additions have occurred when, through study and discovery, it was determined that names deserved to be placed on the wall. More often today, names added are of veterans who have recently died as a direct result of combat-related injuries received in the war. When the occasion arises, new names are etched into the wall around Memorial Day in the spring or Veterans Day in the fall. Since the names on the wall are listed chronologically according to casualty date and because space on the wall is limited, the new names are added as close as possible to the appropriate place where space allows.

Should a service member who is listed as missing-in-action on the wall ever return alive, a circle would be inscribed around the cross next to his name. To date, no such symbols are on the wall.

As concrete was being poured for the foundation of the Vietnam Veterans Memorial, a U.S. Navy officer walked up to the edge of the trench. He paused, threw something in, and saluted. It was his dead brother's Purple Heart. It was also the first offering left at the wall.

Who would have guessed that the Vietnam Veterans Memorial would become an altar of sorts—a place where people would leave offerings of love and remembrance? Who could have known that this Purple Heart would be the first of tens of thousands of items left at the wall? The park rangers and volunteers who worked at the wall knew only that the special objects had to be saved. This was the beginning of the Vietnam Veterans Memorial Collection.

This collection is unlike any museum collection anywhere. Among the artifacts are photographs, letters, MIA/POW bracelets, medals, helmets, dog tags, boots, canned food, unopened beer cans, cigarettes, birthday cards, toys, and bullets. Soldiers who returned home leave objects for those who did not. Many objects are from parents, spouses, siblings, and children. Some offerings are direct communications between the living and the dead; tangible bonds between those who were killed and those who remember. They tell us something about the people on the wall; but as well as any history book, they tell us about an era.

The Vietnam Veterans Memorial Collection was

developed to preserve this special memorabilia. The collection is unique in that a museum curator chooses nothing. Those who lived through this turbulent time in American history choose many of these artifacts.

Each day, park rangers collect the offerings, place them in individual bags, and tag them with the date, a description, and the number of the panel under which the offering was left. They are then transferred to a large storage facility about 12 miles from the wall. There, the items are carefully organized and preserved. The artifacts are so socially and historically significant that the Smithsonian Museum of American History has a large sample of the collection on display. Through these high-

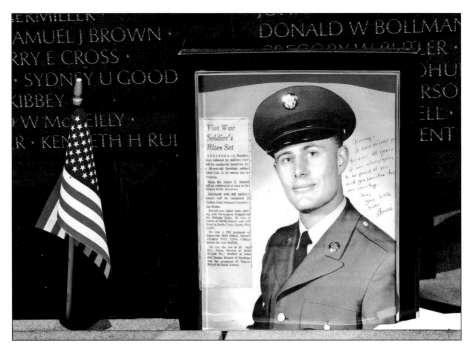

Over the years, more than 400,000 photos, flags, medals, and other items have been left at the wall.

Make Connections

The walls of the memorial are 246.75 feet long and the angle where they come together is 125 degrees, 12 minutes. There are 140 pilings with the average depth to bedrock 35 feet. The height of the walls at the vertex is 10.1 feet.

ly personal messages from the living to the dead, visitors will be able to see, for centuries to come, the impact of the Vietnam War on this country.

Why do people leave these offerings? The reasons behind them are as varied as the items themselves. Men pay off old debts, leaving dollars, cigarettes, and cans of beer. A woman left two sonograms for the grandfather her children would never know. A park ranger tells the story of another woman who left her wedding ring at the wall. She was getting remarried the next day and wanted to say goodbye to, and let go of, her first husband, who had died in Vietnam.

Perhaps the letters and cards say the most. Their words portray feelings of rage, despair, loneliness, loss, and guilt. People leave cards for birthdays, Father's Day, and other holidays. But by communicating with loved ones through the wall, people are able to confront feelings they may have *repressed* for years. They can make peace with themselves and others as pain and guilt are released.

Over the years, the letters are increasingly revealing love, forgiveness, and hope. In this way, the Vietnam Veterans Memorial is much more than a way to honor those men and women who served their country. It has become a way for a whole nation to heal.

Today, the VVMF collaborates with the National Park Service to conduct ceremonies at the memorial on Memorial Day and Veterans Day, to add those names of military personnel who are determined to have died as a result of their service in Southeast Asia during the Vietnam War, to keep records of those listed on the wall, and to maintain residual funds for the maintenance and repair of the memorial.

In 1984, former Army nurse and Vietnam veteran Diane Carlson Evans founded the Vietnam Women's Memorial Project to honor the more than 265,000 women who served during the war, including 10,000 in Vietnam. After a nine-year struggle, a monument to the women who served in Vietnam was constructed. just a few hundred yards away from the wall. The women's memorial features a sculpture by Glenna Goodacre that shows three Vietnam-era women in battle dress. While one nurse cares for a wounded soldier, another kneels in thought or prayer. The third looks to the skies–for help from a helicopter or, perhaps, from a higher power. Goodacre left the interpretation open so that people could read into it whatever

Make Connections

Since the Vietnam Veterans Memorial was dedicated, names have been added to the wall and changes made to the existing names. Originally the wall contained 57,939 names. The wall today has more than 58,200 names.

they wish. The bronze sculpture is almost seven feet tall and weighs 2,000 pounds.

Support for the women's memorial came from all over. Letters pored in from both male and female veterans. Nurses spoke of the horrors of war. Veterans remembered the nurses with love and affection–the kind smile, the gentle touch, and the soft words that eased

VITAL FIGURE: Glenna Goodacre, sculptor

Glenna Goodacre was born in 1939 in Lubbock, Texas. She graduated from Colorado College and studied at the Art Students League in New York before beginning a successful career as a painter and sculptor.

Since the Vietnam Women's Memorial was installed on the National Mall in 1993, the bronze sculpture has been seen by millions of visitors to Washington and has been filmed and photographed extensively by the media.

Before creating the women's memorial, however, Goodacre enjoyed a successful 20-year career as an artist. Known for her portrait busts and figures and for her interesting sculptural compositions of active children, Goodacre also had a successful career as a painter.

Goodacre has more than 40 bronze portraits in public collections in the United States, including sculptures of Dwight D. Eisenhower, Barbara Jordan, Katherine Anne Porter, Lt. Karl W. Richter, Dr. Norris Bradbury, Greer Garson, and Gen. Harry H. "Hap" Arnold. She also has created a seven-foot standing portrait of former President Ronald Reagan for the National Cowboy Hall of Fame and designed the front of a gold-colored dollar coin depicting Shoshoni guide Sacagawea and her infant son, which circulated from 2002 until 2012.

Goodacre divides her time between Santa Fe, New Mexico, where she has maintained a studio since 1983, and Dallas, Texas, where her husband has a law practice.

The Vietnam Women's Memorial honors the American women who served in the conflict.

their pain. Without the nurses, Evans felt, the Vietnam Veterans Memorial wall would have stretched for 50 miles.

In November 1993, the Vietnam Women's Memorial was dedicated, just a few hundred feet from the wall.

Text-Dependent Questions
How many American women served in the military during the years that the U.S. was involved in the Vietnam War? How many actually served in Vietnam?

Research Project
Go to http://vietvet.org/letters.htm to read some letters written during the Vietnam War by American soldiers. What are some similarities between the letters? What are some of the differences?

Chronology

1975 The Army of North Vietnam captures Saigon on April 30; South Vietnam surrenders, ending the war and reunifying the country under Communist control.

1979 Vietnam War veteran Jan Scruggs conceives the idea for a memorial to honor those who served in Vietnam.

1980 On April 30, Congress votes in favor of giving the Vietnam Veterans Memorial Fund two acres of land near the Lincoln Memorial; President Jimmy Carter signs a bill giving VVMF the land on July 1.

1981 Maya Ling Yin's design is selected from 1,421 entries to be constructed as the Vietnam Veterans Memorial.

1982 Construction of the memorial begins in March; it is dedicated on November 13.

1984 Diane Carlson Evans starts the Vietnam Women's Memorial Project.

1986 Fundraising for the VWMP begins.

1988 President Ronald Reagan signs a bill in November to authorize the Vietnam Women's Memorial.

1991 Sculptor Glenna Goodacre is selected to design the women's memorial.

1993 The Vietnam Women's Memorial is dedicated in November.

2004 A plaque honoring veterans who died after the war as a direct result of injuries suffered in Vietnam, but who are not eligible to be listed on the Wall, is unveiled.

2010 After six weeks of restoration work, the Three Servicemen statue is unveiled July 8 during a rededication ceremony.

2012 The Vietnam Veterans Memorial Fund announces that it will put up a display near the Wall honoring American soldiers who served in Iraq and Afghanistan.

2014 More than 4.4 million people visit the Vietnam Wall.

Series Glossary of Key Terms

capstone—a stone used at the top of a wall or other structure.

cornerstone—the first stone placed at a spot where two walls meet, usually considered the starting point of construction.

dome—an element of architecture that resembles the hollow upper half of a sphere.

edifice—a large building with an imposing appearance.

facade—the decorative front of a building.

foundation—the stone and mortar base built below ground that supports a building, bridge, monument, or other structure.

hallowed—holy, consecrated, sacred, or revered.

keystone—the architectural piece at the crown of a vault or arch which marks its apex, locking the other pieces into position.

memorial—something designed to help people remember a person or event in history.

obelisk—a shaft of stone that tapers at the peak.

pantheon—a public building containing monuments to a nation's heroes.

pedestal—the base or support on which a statue, obelisk, or column is mounted.

portico—a roof supported by columns, usually extending out from a building.

rotunda—a large and high circular hall or room in a building, usually surmounted by a dome.

standard—a flag or banner that is adopted as an emblem or symbol by a nation.

symbol—an item that represents or stands for something else.

Further Reading

Axelrod, Alan. *The Real History of the Vietnam War: A New Look at the Past.* New York: Sterling, 2013.

Hamill, Pete. *Vietnam: The Real War: A Photographic History by the Associated Press.* New York: Harry N. Abrams, 2013.

Karnow, Stanley. *Vietnam: A History.* New York: Penguin, 1997.

Meyer, Peter. *The Wall: A Day at the Vietnam Veterans Memorial.* New York: Thomas Dunne Books, 1993.

Morrissey, Thomas F. *Between the Lines: Photographs from the National Vietnam Veterans Memorial.* Syracuse, N.Y.: Syracuse University Press, 2000.

Schaefer, Ted. *The Vietnam Veterans Memorial.* North Mankato, Minn.: Heinemann Library, 2005.

Scruggs, Jan, and Joel L. Swerdlow. *To Heal a Nation.* New York: Harper and Row, 1985.

Sofarelli, Michael. *Letters on the Wall: Offerings and Remembrances from the Vietnam Veterans Memorial.* Washington, D.C.: Smithsonian Books, 2006.

Wiest, Andrew. *Vietnam: A View from the Front Lines.* New York: Osprey Publishing, 2013.

Internet Resources

http://www.vvmf.org

Website of the Vietnam Veterans Memorial Fund (VVMF), the nonprofit organization that funded the memorial. The organization's current initiative is a campaign to build an Education Center at the memorial that will show pictures and tell stories of the soldiers killed in Vietnam, as well as display some of the more than 400,000 items left at the memorial.

http://www.nps.gov/vive/index.htm

National Park Service website for the Vietnam Veterans Memorial includes information about the Wall, the Three Servicemen statue, and the Vietnam Women's Memorial.

http://www.themovingwall.org/

Website of the "Moving Wall," a half-size replica of the Vietnam Veterans Memorial that has been exhibited around the country for almost 30 years.

http://www.usa.gov/visitors/about.shtml

This page provided by the U.S. government gives visitors an opportunity to learn about the United States of America, including links to information about patriotic symbols, American culture and history, government departments and agencies, and other interesting information.

Index

Index

Picture Credits

Contributors

BARRY MORENO has been librarian and historian at the Ellis Island Immigration Museum and the Statue of Liberty National Monument since 1988. *The Statue of Liberty Encyclopedia* (2000), *The Encyclopedia of Ellis Island* (2004), *Ellis Island's Famous Immigrants* (2008), and *The Ellis Island Quiz Book* (2011). He also co-edited a scholarly study on world migration called *Leaving Home: Migration Yesterday and Today* (2011). His biography has been included in *Who's Who Among Hispanic Americans*, *The Directory of National Park Service Historians*, *Who's Who in America*, and *The Directory of American Scholars*. Mr. Moreno lives in New York City.

JOSEPH FERRY is a veteran journalist who has written for several newspapers in Philadelphia and the surrounding suburbs. He lives in Sellersville, Pennsylvania, with his wife and three children. His other books in Mason Crest's PATRIOTIC SYMBOLS OF AMERICA series are *American Flag: The Story of Old Glory, Jefferson Memorial: A Monument to Greatness, and The Star-Spangled Banner: Story of Our National Anthem.*